Romantic STYLE

Romantic
STYLE

Authorized ♔ *Purveyors*

VICTORIA'S SECRET

Nº 10 MARGARET STREET · LONDON W1

Copyright © Victoria's Secret and
George Weidenfeld & Nicolson Ltd, London 1990
First published in 1990
by Victoria's Secret,
10 Margaret Street, London W1N 7LF
and George Weidenfeld & Nicolson Ltd,
91 Clapham High Street, London SW4 7TA

Design Harry Green
Picture research Juliet Brightmore
Text Denny Hemming

Printed and bound in Italy.

Pages 2/3: Dressing-table vignette (Victoria's Secret)
Endpapers, pages 1, 4/5: a design for
a printed calico, c. 1780
(Musée de l'Impression sur Etoffes de Mulhouse)

CONCEIVED AND DESIGNED
IN LONDON
BY VICTORIA'S SECRET

CONTENTS

A HINT
OF
ROMANCE

The creation of a truly romantic room requires a certain felicitous abandon, for romantic style is essentially a personal fantasy, and as such it lies in the eye of the beholder. For some the romantic illusion recalls the nostalgia of Victorian England, a world filled with lace and roses; for others it is the theatrical opulence of the Arabian Nights replete with tented boudoirs. But romance can equally be conjured by a certain rustic simplicity evoked by attic rooms tucked under snug eaves, by roses around a cottage door, the whole suffused by the romantic innocence of the pastoral idyll. Then there are those country-house drawing-rooms that epitomize a very English form of romanticism with their assured and serene way of life. There are bedrooms that provide an escape from the outside world, dining-rooms for intimate candlelit entertainment and conservatories that provide a cool, flower-filled retreat from the heat of a summer's day.

The walls of any home, no matter how modest, can contain illusions no matter how grand. Rural escapism can be given full reign in a city apartment with a mural depicting a pastoral scene, for *trompe l'oeil* is literally a deception of the eye. But unlike so many romantic dreams, it will not fade away. If by chance you desire a panorama of rolling countryside or of picturesque ruins, peopled with lovers arm-in-arm beside sparkling fountains, all are attainable through the skilful brushwork of illusion.

Romantic associations with the past offer enormous scope for self-indulgence. Favourite elements from different centuries can be re-arranged according to personal whim. Artful deception heightens romantic style. But romance has touched certain periods more than others. Few have taken it to more capricious extremes than the Rococo with its cupids, shells, flowers and spangles. This effusively pretty style emerged in the wake of the Baroque which melted into the frills and furbelows of this most boudoir style of decoration. Beds became confections of silk and satin; curved mouldings and ornament decorated furniture; nymphs and satyrs, shepherds and shepherdesses inhabited the furnishings, all reflected in gilded mirrors and brought to life by candlelight.

The English love of the whimsical was also captivated by the Orient, in particular the cult of chinoiserie and its evocation of far-off lands. A brief dalliance with the exoticism of India followed with the onion domes of the Prince Regent's Pavilion. Here was a world that Marco Polo knew centuries before – a world of silk and spice routes, of rich lustre and glowing colour. The tent room, at first a male preserve associated with the campaign tent and the exploits of Napoleon, was soon in demand with pleated ceilings and fabric walls conjuring all the languorous exoticism of the East.

The romance of medieval England was heralded by the fairytale battlements and crenellations of the Gothic, imbued with an aura of romantic chivalry that is a recurrent theme of English literature. The Gothic, with its follies such as Strawberry Hill – the epitome of romantic escapism – stands for the dramatic side of the style, but the allure of each historical interlude resides in a sense of a different time and place, a transportation, a suspension of reality.

There is also a particularly English romantic style that revolves around nature, the romantic sweetness of flowers as a symbol of innocence. The cultivation of flowers was pursued both outside and inside the home, and a profusion of floral motifs spread over chintzes and sprigged cotton, over wallpaper and across carpets. Flowers have

always been associated with romantic love at its most lyrical. Until the end of the Victorian age, lovers would send each other bunches of flowers from which a message could be read according to its arrangement.

Locations play their part in the romantic setting, too, for it is not only a question of decoration within the walls but also what nature has provided beyond. To look out upon a panorama which prompts immediate visual pleasure is uplifting for the spirits. Imagine flinging open French windows onto a meadow filled with wild flowers – instantly the room takes on a more captivating appeal. Or waking up to a sea view with breakers frothing foam upon the silver sands below. Romance is inherent in a setting of natural splendour, whether it is by a lake accompanied by the sound of lapping water, a hillside stained mauve with heather or a bluff overlooking a harbour, which by night glitters with twinkling lights from homecoming fishing boats.

Romantic style derives inspiration from the arts – from painting, poetry and music. The Romantic artist explored the values of intuition and instinct, a more private kind of expression that flowered in the works of Wordsworth, Byron, Shelley and Keats. Watteau's paintings of *fêtes galantes* have the same lightness and sharpness as a Mozart

An air of expectation presides over this romantic scene, the setting perhaps for a summer wedding breakfast. Looking through the classical doorway the view is an essay in pale sophistication. An antique lace cloth is draped over the table, its centrepiece a pair of silver candlesticks, while above it a crystal chandelier adds to the grand spectacle. An extravagant bouquet of fragrant cream roses and delicate white lilac awaits the bride.

opera, the same understanding, too, of the drama of human relationships. Romance feeds on allusion and of all the arts, music is arguably the most evocative, setting a mood, lulling the senses and providing an aura of tranquillity. It has an unrivalled power to summon up places long forgotten or fond memories, its notes entangled in the fabric of the emotions. Its potent quality has been remarked upon from Shakespeare to Noel Coward. Lovers have serenaded each other with music for centuries. Many an eighteenth-century boudoir would have had a pretty harpsichord in one corner for after-dinner entertainment while the paintings of Tissot a century later capture the atmosphere of Parisian soirées at which music provides a truly romantic accompaniment to the occasion.

In creating the romantic *mise en scène*, a number of elements are at your disposal. Colour and fabric are the magic wand with which transformation scenes can be achieved. The key is in taking an idea to extremes: swathes of chintz, with its soft sheen, create a romantic ambience when draped about a French window; delicate lace, used to cocoon the private world of the four-poster, imbues a room with romantic femininity; an attic bedroom can be washed in pale ice-cream colours of rose pink and pale green; or an intimate dining-room given dramatic allure by painting it midnight blue. Flowers bring an instant aura of romance to a room, recreating the air of a spring morning or a summer's day, and the attraction of firelight on a winter's evening or candlelight reflected in sparkling mirrors has never been surpassed.

In the same way that a playwright sets the scene for a romantic encounter, manipulating the emotions of the onlooker and bringing about the desired reactions, a room can set the scene for the fantasies of its creator.

ELEMENTS OF MAGIC

You remember our dear little house in Curzon Street; when we furnished it, nothing would please us but watered paper on the walls, garlands of roses tied with blue bows!

LADY MOUNT TEMPLE, *Memorials*

CELESTIAL BLUE

The colour blue instantly conjures images of sky and ocean, which by their very sense of infinity are a balm to the spirit: the pale blue-grey of dawn, the translucent azure of limpid waters, the grape-blue of impending storms, the deep velvety damson-blue of a summer's night – its shades are limitless. Blue is 'darkness made visible', that magic moment of the evening when the very air takes on a certain hue.

The classic French perfume L'Heure Bleu takes its name from this intensely romantic hour between dusk and darkness, a time when traditionally ladies entertained their lovers and men called on their mistresses.

Blue occurs throughout nature – in blue eyes, peacocks' feathers, dragonflies' wings. Flowers have lent their names to a particular shade: woodlands are filled with shady drifts of blue-bells, violets are naturalized under a canopy of trees, not to mention the heavy boughs of lilac blossom and seas of forget-me-nots – the colour blue stretches from tones of celestial delicacy to incomparable richness.

Blue is found in the swirling hues of lapis lazuli and the brilliant tones of sapphire. Peacock blue was first imported into Venice from China in the form of blue-green iridescent silks which graced European drawing-rooms in the seventeenth and eighteenth centuries, while the delicate

17

Chinoiserie has been the inspiration for this cool drawing-room with its air of sophistication. The overall effect is one of intensity, of blue-on-blue, achieved through a subtle interrelationship of pattern, texture and fabric. It is a room that recalls the atmosphere of French Empire style with its vivid colour, striped walls, bold reefed curtain and elegant bolstered daybed inviting hours of indulgent relaxation. Enhanced by the natural light that floods through from French windows, this blue colour scheme takes on a truly luminous quality.

porcelain from the royal factory of Sèvres in France was to become prized for its sky-blue colour. Artists, too, have been drawn to this mystical hue, notably Picasso for whom blue was the colour 'that exists best in the world . . . the colour of all colours, the bluest of all blues.'

A setting in shades of blue creates an atmosphere of deep serenity. It can act as a soothing backdrop or provide a subtle accent colour in a decorative scheme, adding depth, quietude or a flash of colour according to the shade. While a single-colour scheme effectively unifies the elements of a room, contrast in the form of texture, tone and pattern provides interest for the eye. Nor does such a scheme ever remain one colour for long, for natural light changes hues from hour to hour.

Comfort is an indispensable element of romantic style and a capacious armchair is the perfect place in which to curl up with a novel or long-awaited letter. A panoply of down-filled cushions, round and frilled, lace-covered or embroidered, and heaped in generous array, creates an instantly inviting corner. A silk shawl thrown over the back or arm of a chair adds an extra feminine touch.

In a country living-room, blue in its palest shade of silvery slate washes over the interior landscape to give a soft, hazy, restful atmosphere that is echoed in fabrics, such as a dusky blue-and-cream damask and a faded floral chintz. The blue-grey marble of the fireplace picks up the theme together with the pastel lampshades. It is a composition that captures the translucent quality of early morning light. But blue has a dramatic aspect in the deeper reaches of its character – mysterious violets and velvety indigos that echo the vibrant tones of heavy hydrangea blossoms.

Blue is as natural a companion to white as cream is to coffee. A perennial favourite, such a combination is cool, demure and inviting with a sense of spaciousness and light. Its inspiration derives perhaps from the vogue for chinoiserie beloved of English country houses in the eighteenth century.

A dining-room dictates an air of formality, a sense of occasion. Recreate a print room, once a fashion of the late eighteenth century, and evoke the lyrical dilettante air of the Regency. Prints were pasted straight onto the wall and embellished with ornate printed borders and flourishes of swags and bows. Classical scenes were often used, a reminder of trophies brought back from the Grand Tour. In a dining-room blue can act as a relaxing background colour in paler shades of azure and lavender; it can add drama in deepest midnight blue; or it can provide accent tones in the vivid indigo of Bristol glass. In its myriad guises, blue is the peace-maker of colours: cool and soothing, it creates a halcyon oasis by day or by night.

A GOLDEN GLOW

Yellow is the colour of sunlight, gold and spring flowers; of luscious fruit, of 'amber waves of grain' and sandy shores. Its significance permeates the myths of European folklore in countless tales of flaxen-haired heroines. Equally it is the colour of glowing fires, autumn sunsets and moonlight, of lighted windows at night and the amber gleam of cats' eyes in the dark. It begins subtly with palest primrose deepening to the golden tones of saffron and the richness of tawny ochre and burnt sienna.

Colour is a means of evoking the romance of the past. Apricot and vivid yellow were fashionable colours in the eighteenth century, brought back to England by young aristocrats who had completed the Grand Tour of Europe. Rooms were hung with either paper or silk and gilding brightened every corner.

Such colour schemes work as well in winter, when warm tones provide a glowing contrast to the stark landscape outside, as they do in summer when such a room can seem almost the extension of a sun-filled garden. Take an old-fashioned shrub-rose garden as inspiration, with its multi-coloured petals of yellow, apricot, pink, red and white. Translated into deep chintz-covered sofas or curtains of pale yellow and green silk this will make for a most romantic setting.

Full many a glorious morning have I seen

Flatter the mountain-tops with sovereign eye,

Kissing with golden face the meadows green,

Gilding pale streams with heavenly alchymy.

SHAKESPEARE, *Sonnets* (33)

CREAM & LACE

Lace is inherently the most romantic of fabrics, and supremely feminine. Teamed with cream silk, it makes for an air of unabashed luxury. Whether lace takes centre stage as a lavish canopy over a four-poster bed, creating a picture of fairytale romance, or whether it forms a finishing touch to freshly laundered sheets as a delicate edging, it adds a sense of extravagance.

Made of cotton or linen threads, sometimes silk, lace is traditionally produced in tones of ivory or white, but it can be dyed any shade. Handmade lace is still a luxury, but loom lace can look just as attractive, the best-known varieties including Nottingham lace, woven on a jacquard loom, and Madras lace of gauze-like lightness. The charm of the fabric lies in its pattern-

A mirror image, past and present, capturing the nostalgic mood of the pastoral idyll. A country bedroom, nestling under the eaves, has an in-built aura of romance. Irregular walls are sprinkled with tangled nosegays of hedgerow flowers, effectively camouflaging odd nooks and crannies. A Victorian jug and basin forms a decorative feature, rather than a practical necessity, on a washstand backed with a soft drape of gathered lace, an echo of the pretty bedspread tucked over the Victorian brass bed. A dress of antique lace is laid out in anticipation of a special occasion.

ing, ranging from Rococo filigree or floral posies and bows to large-scale motifs, and its soft drape.

Windows are a superb opportunity for pure romance with full-length undercurtains billowing in a gentle breeze; or draped with a soft pelmet of lace looped over a decorative pole; or covered with a flat lace panel that simulates the delicate effect of etched glass. The Regency favoured lace in its window schemes with lengths of the fabric reefed up Empire-style, a reflection of the costume fashions of the day with their high waistlines. An extravagant effect used in Victorian interiors incorporates several layers of ivory lace, edged with a silk bobble fringe and caught up at intervals with silk rosettes to create a shimmering effect that exploits the light-filtering quality of this luxurious fabric to the full.

White lace hung over pink silk walls was an elaboration of the Rococo, utterly feminine in both treatment and colour scheme and an effect that can be recreated today with a frieze of lace at cornice level that allows the background colour to peep through. A dressing table, decked out with a generous skirt of lace over plain or figured silk and given additional ruffles and bows, echoes the frothy confections favoured in the eighteenth-century boudoir, in which a fichu of lace also framed the table mirror. Silver-topped scent bottles and brushes complete the picture.

Lace is a hallmark of the nostalgia for Victoriana and for the old-world romance of a country lifestyle. The traditional pretti-ness of a bedroom is enhanced with lace-edged bedcovers and pillows or by lacy cloths over bedside tables, used perhaps over a floral chintz and caught up at intervals like a skirt revealing its petticoats. The romantic touch of gathered lace used as a valance along a mantelpiece softens the contours of a fireplace, a decidedly feminine arrangement.

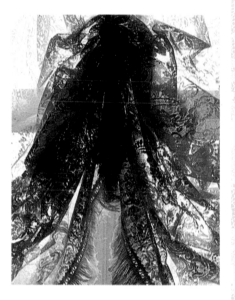

The bed itself is a wonderful opportunity for indulgence. A spritz of lace flung over a pole can create a simple canopy; hung from a central corona, swathes of cream silk can be twisted around each corner of the bed, perhaps decorated with ribbons and bows, to achieve a lighter but equally sumptuous variant on the traditional drapery for a four-poster bed. Or enclose a bed *en niche* in the eighteenth-century manner with screens of lace to create a cocoon of seclusion.

Only the most delicate, floral-patterned china will comple-ment a lace tablecloth laid for afternoon tea, a scene which recaptures the spirit of a past age. Silver looks at its best against lace runners on a dining-room sideboard. As a finishing touch lace cushions, lined with a darker silk or glazed cotton to show up their detail, thrown on a garden seat will summon up that sense of romantic extravagance that lace embodies.

SHADES OF GREEN

The mind, that ocean where each kind
Does straight its own resemblance find;
Yet it creates, transcending these,
Far other worlds, and other seas;
Annihilating all that's made
To a green thought in a green shade.

ANDREW MARVELL, *The Garden*

Green is a fresh, cool and natural colour; it conjures the velvety splendour of a well-kept lawn, silvery-green willow branches arched over sun-dappled water, the invigorating scent of wet pine needles. It is the colour of the emerald and the pale gleam of copper domes and spires on the horizon. It is the colour of the planet Venus, and therefore of love itself.

Various shades of green have gone in and out of fashion over the centuries. The Georgians imported the bright apple-green from France which was to be a favourite until later in the eighteenth century, when it gave way to the paler pistachio hues of Robert Adam, in whose schemes cool green tones, offset by white and pastel pink, created an aura of romance.

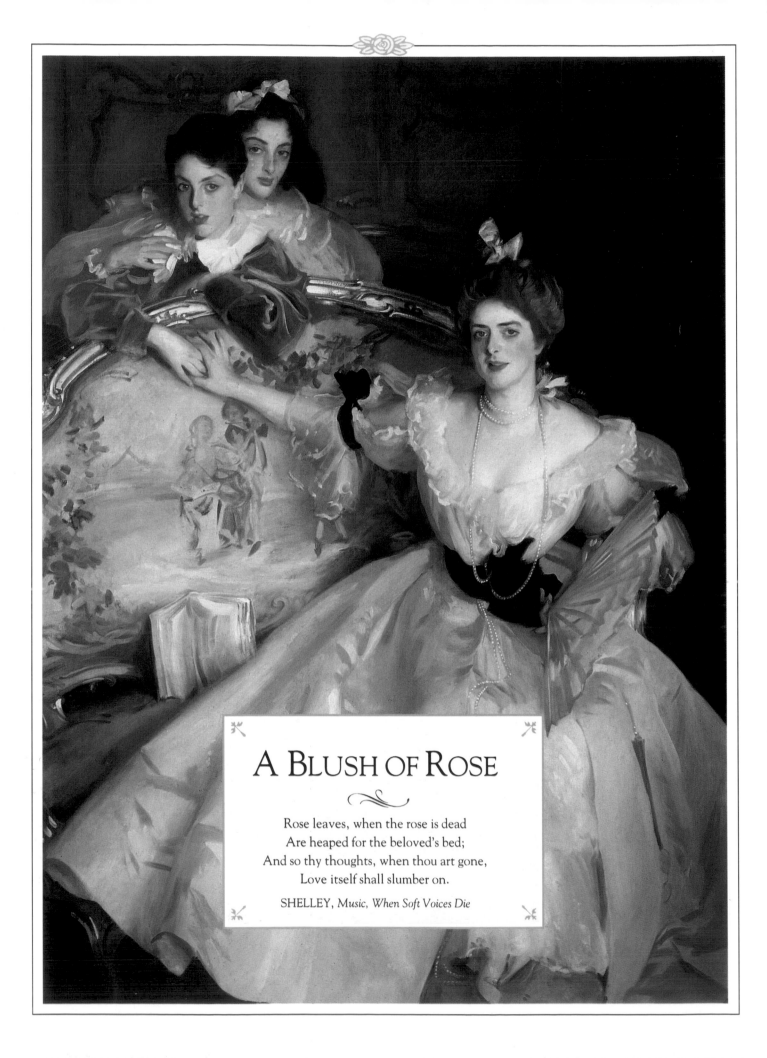

A BLUSH OF ROSE

Rose leaves, when the rose is dead
Are heaped for the beloved's bed;
And so thy thoughts, when thou art gone,
Love itself shall slumber on.

SHELLEY, *Music, When Soft Voices Die*

Think of pink and the delicate hues of wild roses, meander through the velvety hybrids to warm coral and shocking fuchsia, to the rich ruby of jewels and the dark sheen of plums and grapes. As palest pink the character of this colour is feminine, gentle but vibrant; as sumptuous red it is associated with passion and the heart, a motif that graced every nineteenth-century Valentine's Day card in Victorian England.

Pink, used layer upon layer, shade upon shade, creates a warm, glowing atmosphere. Candy-pink stripes, with their allusion to sweet confectionery and Brighton Rock, will create a romantic vista when used as full-length curtains to frame a view

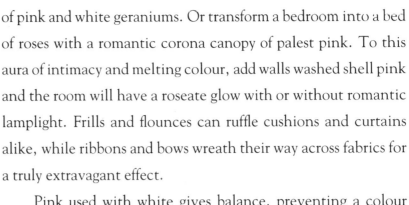

of pink and white geraniums. Or transform a bedroom into a bed of roses with a romantic corona canopy of palest pink. To this aura of intimacy and melting colour, add walls washed shell pink and the room will have a roseate glow with or without romantic lamplight. Frills and flounces can ruffle cushions and curtains alike, while ribbons and bows wreath their way across fabrics for a truly extravagant effect.

Pink used with white gives balance, preventing a colour scheme from looking too cloying. Used as an accent colour in flowers or cushions, pink will take the edge off cool pastel greens or blues. Fill a little Victorian grate with dried flowers in shades of pink to recall summer days, or smother a bed with pink cushions in a range of shapes, sizes and fabrics – silks, lace and delicate embroidery – for sheer indulgence.

EXOTIC
TAPESTRY

I magine a Persian carpet in jewel-like colours, antique gold and crimson embroidered cushions piled high upon an inviting
ottoman, trimmed with lavish fringes and
tassels and mellowed by centuries of time and
use, the whole confection capped by a tented
ceiling of gathered silk. This is romance of a
different kind, opulent and redolent of far-off
lands and tales of Arabian Nights.

A sumptuous sense of texture has given tapestry and rich embroidery a sensuous appeal for centuries. In Elizabethan England lavish textiles, once the province of the church, moved into the realm of secular warmth and opulence. Prized Oriental carpets, the result of trade with the exotic East and crusading zeal, covered tables while silks, velvets and fine embroidery, spangled with gold and silver, were used for wall and bed hangings. The Rococo brought chinoiserie tapestries and a lighter, more frivolous look. Scenes of dalliance, embroidered on silk, brought romance to the bedroom while the muted pinks and golds of Aubusson carpets, spattered with roses, covered the floors of the *salons*.

The rich colours of tartan too conjure a romantic vision as portrayed in the swashbuckling novels of Sir Walter Scott, with their scenes of turreted castles, shrouded in mist, and pipers on the ramparts at dawn. Tartans bear the evocative names of warring clans such as Macpherson, Mackenzie and Royal Stewart. By a massive fireplace and surrounded by thick stone walls adorned with antlers, ancient tartans in glowing colours of crimson, forest-green, indigo and black have a dark romance all their own.

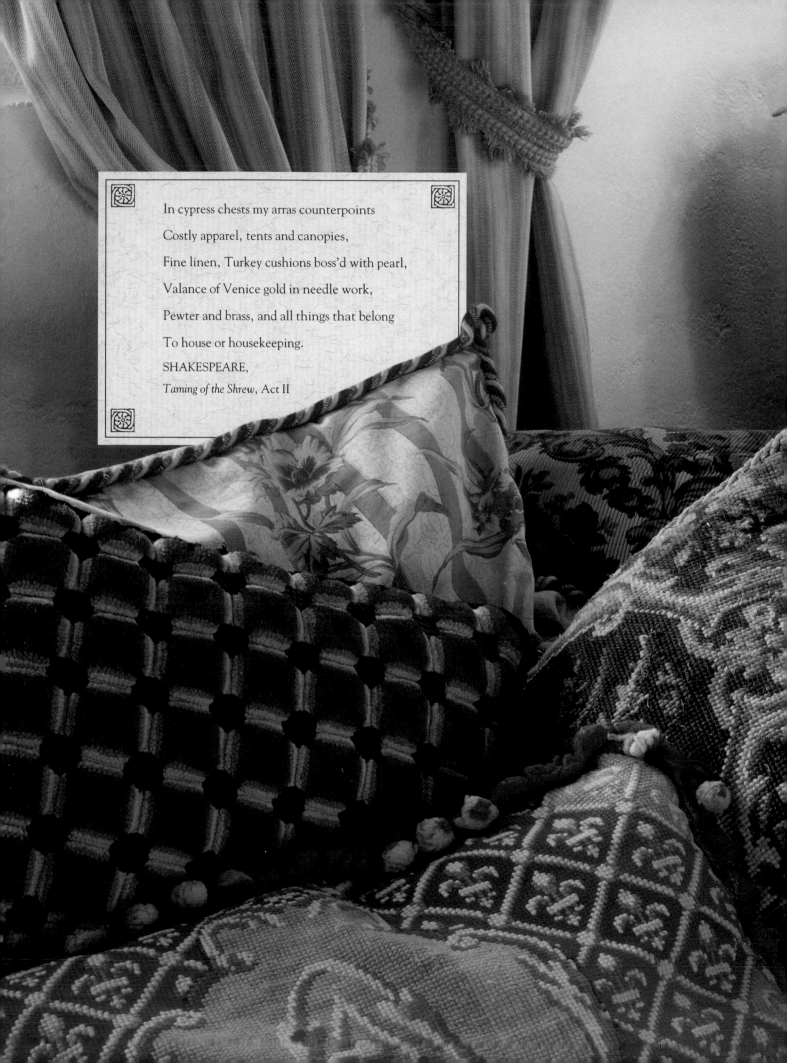

In cypress chests my arras counterpoints

Costly apparel, tents and canopies,

Fine linen, Turkey cushions boss'd with pearl,

Valance of Venice gold in needle work,

Pewter and brass, and all things that belong

To house or housekeeping.

SHAKESPEARE,

Taming of the Shrew, Act II

LIGHT & SHADE

◦~◦

Summer rooms come into their own when filled with sunlight. Other rooms work best in winter when feelings of warmth prevail. But romance is most in favour after sundown when open fires and candlelight, reflected in sparkling mirrors, provide the most evocative backdrop of all.

The decorative nature of natural light can be orchestrated according to mood by means of lace curtains, blinds and shutters, all of which enhance atmosphere by filtering light in a softer, more flattering way. Period details also have their effect: lattice windows cast graphic shadows upon mellow stonework, and stained glass, so beloved of the Victorians, creates pools of jewel-like colour.

Daylight, with its constantly changing nuances, gives life to an interior. Every day there are a thousand subtle ways in which natural light shows up colours, shapes and textures. It is this variety which delights the eye. The low sun at dusk or dawn has golden, rosy tints; at noon on a clear day the sun casts bright shafts of light coupled with strong, direct shadows whereas light filtered through clouds has a soft, even tone. And light varies in different parts of the world and according to the seasons, a quality long appreciated by artists.

The aspect of a room affects its character. A morning room, once a feature of the eighteenth-century home, takes advantage of early light to provide an intimate sunlit haven in which to take breakfast or write letters. Conversely, an introspective room with little natural light will come into its own after dark. It is these extremes of day and night that create a transformation scene within one's four walls.

Lighting can bring a room to life, giving it a sense of theatre, of space sculptured with light and shade, or it can make surroundings softer and more flattering with pools of low light and soft shadows. Skilfully arranged, artificial lighting can be manipulated to adjust the shape and size of a room, highlighting certain objects or paintings and playing down other areas. Lighting contributes to a room's personality, which is seen at its most compelling at night. Gentle overall light interspersed with areas of brilliance and shade creates a festive chiaroscuro for special occasions and adds vitality. Subtle lighting in a pink room recreates a rosy sunset while glossy lacquered walls are especially effective in candlelight. Mirrors lend added shimmer and dimmer controls allow mood to be modulated at the touch of a switch.

The bedroom is an obvious candidate for skilful, flattering lighting; the living-room is where dramatic lighting is seen at its most persuasive, or perhaps in a dining-room used exclusively for entertaining. The style of lighting, the shapes and colours of lampshades are all important in setting the scene.

Lampshades can be tied in to the room scheme, taking the background colour of a fabric or wallpaper, or perhaps using a stencil motif taken from a border. Coolie shades balance classical column bases while pleated shades in flowered chintz or silk, bound with contrast binding or fan-edged braid, look pretty above a ceramic base as do pleated paper shades with ribbon threaded through top and bottom. Flower motifs pasted onto a shade lightly echo the scrap screens of the Victorian era, while Argand-style oil lamps with their frosted glass globes bring a specific period atmosphere. Cutwork paper shades have a country charm, throwing delicate patterns of light on wall and ceiling. Lined with pink fabric, shades cast an extra soft light.

No one who has ever dined in the room or has even seen it when closed and lit up, can say a word against the almost miraculous beauty of the decoration, which, by artificial light when the shutters which formed an integral part of the scheme were closed, was quite wonderful and entrancing . . .

C. E. WILLIAMSON, *Murray Marks and His Friends*

An open fire has never been excelled as a romantic setting, creating an aura of warmth and intimacy. It has a special quality of light, the chiaroscuro effect of flickering flames and dancing shadows adding an element of theatricality to a fire-lit dinner table, while firelight in a bedroom emanates a relaxed atmosphere, its burning embers glowing in the evening twilight and inviting hours of dreamy contemplation. No wonder that such settings have often formed the backdrop to romantic interludes in literature and poetry.

The hearth has been a potent symbol of protection from the elements, a haven from the world outside, from time immemorial. Despite modern technology, which has rendered the fire as a source of heat unnecessary, the deep-seated need for the warmth and welcome of a romantic fireside continues. The fireplace is still the decorative heart of a room, giving it character and focus. It can be on a grand scale, fashioned of marble and carved in classical vein with swags, festoons and medallions, complemented by overmantel mirrors. A Victorian fireplace has a more cosy appeal with its little cast-iron grate and tiled surround flanked by a copper coal scuttle and toasting forks resting on a curly brass fender, ready to cook muffins for tea on a winter's afternoon. A huge rustic fireplace with deep inglenooks is an all-embracing affair with a vast hearth on which to stretch out and read a favourite novel, savouring the aromatic scent of burning pine boughs and fir cones.

A fire comes into its own at twilight when the sun's rays give way to dusky shadows. For the element of light is as much a part of the romantic *mise en scène* as exotic floral decoration or swathes of sumptuous fabric – never mere illumination, more the setting of a mood.

From the classical sparkle of candlelight reflected in a pretty Rococo mirror to the gentle glimmer from a china chamberstick that lights the way to bed, the romantic ambience of candlelight is unrivalled.

Its soft, subtle effects have graced interiors for centuries. The wealth of a Georgian household was assessed by the number of candles that were lit for receptions and balls and family pride was maintained by a selection of Waterford glass or branched silver candelabra. Wall sconces lit richly furnished rooms; placed symmetrically between windows backed by mirror glass or over tables in alcoves, they cast pretty fan shapes of light. Individual candles were used for reading or sewing, sometimes topped with a little parchment shade. But chandeliers were the *pièce de résistance*. Made of glass, small drops were strung around an ormolu frame, reflecting the candles around the perimeter in a glittering cascade of glass.

The romance of candlelight has never gone out of fashion. It remains the most evocative accessory to an intimate dinner party, perhaps continuing the eighteenth-century fashion for little shades so that flames do not dazzle vision. Tall attenuated candle stands, or torchères, impart an Empire atmosphere, the effect enhanced by placing one to either side of a mirror in perfect symmetry. Wall sconces flanking a fireplace heighten a mood of romantic elegance while an antique chandelier catches the spirit of country-house grandeur. Although nothing evokes the past more than candlelight, chandeliers today are usually fitted for electricity, but a sock of pretty fabric in a colour to match the room will disguise the flex and echo past traditions. Or for real flights of fancy adapt a pretty gilded birdcage or fly a Montgolfier-style balloon, fashioned as a chandelier, complete with blue candles. The sky is the limit where fantasy is concerned.

A SENSE OF
OCCASION

Celebrating romantic occasions such as a summer wedding or seasonal festivity provides an opportunity for theatrical effects that set the event apart from everyday life. Interiors, too, can be transformed to enhance the atmosphere.

Dining has always been a ceremonious occasion and needs a romantic ambience to suit. The table setting with its luxurious air of fine china and sparkling glass, an extravagant floral centrepiece, the flattering luminosity of candlelight reflected in an overmantel mirror – all have their part to play in creating an event to remember.

The overall theme can be capricious and feminine in tones of ivory and pink, reflected in the table setting with one tablecloth swagged over another in toning colours and caught with a rosette of fabric. Napkins can be tied with ribbons or flowers in complementary hues. An arrangement of fragrant, full-blown roses can decorate the table or, for a less formal composition, a centrepiece of floating candles interspersed with flowerheads such as pale pink roses and tulips will create a suitably romantic atmosphere. Alternatively, scatter flowers over a damask cloth with felicitous abandon.

A dramatically different environment redolent of Renaissance interiors can be conjured in tones of midnight blue or deepest vermilion with flashes of gold. A bacchanalian pyramid of blue-black grapes and purple plums, liberally frosted with icing sugar and wreathed with ivy, would provide an appropriate focal point.

Candlelight cannot fail to evoke a romantic, indulgent scene, especially when used to excess. Artfully placed mirrors compound the effect, further enhancing the glittering spectacle.

A wedding dress of ivory silk, complete
with matching silk slippers and a bridal
basket of flowers, is laid out
for this the most romantic of occasions.

Of all the events in the course of life a wedding must be the most romantic of all, with visions of lace veils and silk taffeta, showers of rose petals and the strains of Mendelssohn and Purcell. June is the traditional month for weddings. Picture a billowing pavilion lined in stripes of palest pink and white, its tent poles wreathed in flowers and pink ribbons. There is potential magic within its walls as tables are covered in lacy cloths that are pinned, swagged and pleated, and laid with traditional floral arrangements of orange blossom and freesias or little Victorian nosegays with tendrils of ivy. The opportunities for decoration are limitless with no rules other than to be in harmony with the occasion: nostalgic and romantic, simple or grand. The centrepiece of any wedding feast is the tiered cake. Wreathed with old-fashioned roses it is a confection that is irresistible to all the senses.

With the arrival of the Christmas season, rooms made dull by bleak winter light cry out to be given a touch of glamour. Blazing log fires, rich colours and sumptuous decorations welcome family and friends alike. Deck the halls with boughs of holly and balls of mistletoe for seasonal romance. Bring a festive air to rooms with garlands of pine and ivy, entwined with gold ribbon and swagged about mantelpieces or twisted through bannisters. A parade of candles of all shapes and sizes will fill the room with their soft gleam, drawing out the pungent scent of pine needles. But most magical of all is the Christmas tree itself, dressed from top to toe with glittering baubles for this festive occasion.

FLOWERS &
FRAGRANCE

Flowers link the interior to the world outside by reflecting the mood of different seasons and landscapes, while fragrance from the sensuous richness of roses and lilies to the humble charm of the country nosegay conjures a wealth of romantic association.

Country flowers reflect the seasons in a pastoral array of tulips, sprays of cherry blossom and sprigs of forget-me-not that epitomise spring, while the delicate fronds of Queen Anne's lace and fragrant philadelphus, contrasting with the verdant foliage of maple twigs, herald the warm days of summer. Arranged in a Victorian jug and basin on a starched lace runner, country flowers add just the right note of rustic charm.

Fragrant flowers are a feast for all the senses, and none more so than those from an English country garden which have an innocence and freshness all their own. Armfuls of honeysuckle, night-scented stocks and wallflowers will fill the air with a nostalgic mixture of summery scents and will delight the eye with a palette of soft, rain-washed colours. Pretty Victorian pitchers brimming with sweetpeas or the tumbling spires of lilac can be married with plants from the hedgerows – meadow rue with its delicate tracery or Queen Anne's lace. Sweet-smelling herbs, too, will provide a fragrant framework into which a tapestry of country flowers can be woven.

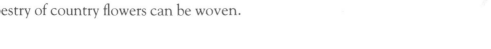

Throughout history flowers have been picked from gardens and strewn upon walls, on fabrics and carpets alike. The floral motif is without doubt the best loved of interior designers. Natural flowers, painted flowers, dried flowers – each epoque treats them in its own way: chintzes over which roses ramble in shades of pink and cream, wallpapers with little sprigs and posies, dower chests stencilled with garlands of flowers, even fantasy gardens painted *trompe l'oeil* onto the walls. Complementing such a theme with real flowers can convey a total mood whether it is one of romantic splendour or country-cottage charm.

Equally, flowers can be used in deliberate contrast to the colours and patterns of a decorative scheme, giving new life to surroundings and creating unexpected accents. A restricted palette of a single colour such as yellow in a neutral setting will radiate vitality; vivid red flowers advance and seen against dark green leaves will glow like jewels while blue flowers, by a window, will lead the eye on to the garden beyond.

The very word pot-pourri conjures images of an English country-house drawing-room, mellow with afternoon sun and filled with the lingering scent of rose, lavender and lemon verbena from a bowl brimful of fragrant petals. Recipes for these floral conceits, blended with spices and perfumed oils, were passed down from generation to generation, with each room of the house allotted its own special concoction: the sweet musky scent of Old English rose for a bedroom, tangy citrus for a panelled library or a mélange of cottage-garden petals for a morning room. A pot-pourri can be full of cherished memories, too, by preserving the centrepiece from a dinner party, a birthday bouquet or the first flowers of spring.

Dried flower displays can range from magnificent floral decorations of pale cream and apricot roses and chrysanthemums, which draw inspiration from Dutch flower paintings, to an informal arrangement in a country basket – roses, Michaelmas daisies and grasses in cottage-garden colours of rose-pink and lavender.

Beautiful as living, fresh bouquets may be, their effect will fade with the flowers themselves. However, by calling upon the skills of a bygone age we can capture the fragrant moment and carry glorious summer into autumn and winter by preserving flowers to brighten those times of year when the garden slumbers.

Gather flowers after the sun has evaporated the early morning dew, choosing such blooms as peonies and pinks, roses and violets for both colour and fragrance. Ornamental grasses, seed pods and herbs add variety. The simplest way of drying stemmed flowers is to hang them upside down in loose bunches, while delicate petals or flowerheads should be dried on frames of stretched muslin. Fill wicker baskets or porcelain cachepôts with displays that complement the colour scheme and style of a room to provide a lasting reminder of summer days.

Romance is about taking ideas to their limits and flowers come into their own when a bravura effect is required. A wedding is just such an occasion with a lavish all-white display of glorious lilies, roses and gladioli. For less formal events flowers can achieve the same sumptuous effect in a more spontaneous way through colour. In a room washed fuchsia-pink, a crystal vase of pink peonies and antirrhinum reinforces the vibrant theme.

Special occasions cover a wide spectrum of out-of-the-ordinary events ranging from a small dinner party to a wedding reception. At such times, flowers play an important part; they must echo the general mood, even create it. Such circumstances provide excellent opportunities for flights of fancy and floral abundance. A special occasion implies a certain formality. The strength of a formal arrangement comes from extravagant use of materials, its delicacy from the slender silhouette of a rhythmic balanced design, which should harmonize with the architecture of the setting be it an alcove or mantelpiece.

The entrance to a home should greet guests with the pleasure of the unexpected as well as happy memories. Fresh flowers are ideal for bringing that element of change to familiar surroundings. A sense of luxury can be played up in the bedroom by introducing flowers with scented blooms in soft shades that echo the fabrics. Dusky pastels recreate the soft glow of an interior by the French artist Vuillard with pink and white hydrangeas mixed with Queen Anne's lace and pink tassels of bridewort and blue love-in-a-mist. Rounded decorations are appropriate for a dinner table setting where the height of flowers must be limited. For easy unmannered simplicity group a hummock of roses, grape hyacinths, sweet peas, tulips, freesias and peonies in vibrant colours of mauve, pink and apricot in a low porcelain bowl and continue the floral theme in napkins and china.

The forget-me-not symbolises true love.
Two lovers were walking by a river when the
lady admired a flower on an island. Her
bethrothed leapt into the water to pluck it,
but was overcome. He laid the flower at her
feet, murmuring with his dying breath
'Forget me not'.

Living rooms provide the setting for the greatest variety of floral arrangements, offering opportunities for exploring new colours and accenting different features of the room, thus realising its full potential.

Fitting platforms for flowers include side tables, a chest, mantelpiece or windowsill. Tablescapes with their small, still-life collections of treasured possessions can be enhanced by including flowers as part of the arrangement, linked by colour or theme: scented nosegays with a collection of fruitwood or enamelled boxes, a single exotic bloom with mementoes of travels to far-off places. Flowers should be scaled according to the total picture and interesting juxtapositions can be created by combining rough with smooth, simple with ornate.

A fireplace is the focal point that attracts most attention in a room and is an effective area to display flowers, either clustered in groups for an informal effect or, in a more traditional setting, massed as a symmetrical display. If a mirror stands over the fireplace use a pair of beautiful vases to each side with an ornament in the centre. In spring or summer an empty hearth can be covered with a floral screen matched with corresponding flowers on the shelf above.

Lighting has an effect on floral decorations. Species such as tulips will rearrange themselves according to the source of natural light and table lamps will emphasize the delicate hues of flowers placed beneath them – the frilled outline of sweet-pea petals highlighted beneath lamplight makes a romantic addition to any living room.

THE GARDEN BEYOND

❧

W here house meets garden there lies romantic potential, be it a glorious view, a shady terrace or a flower-filled conservatory – the perfect location for afternoon tea. But the most idyllic verdant haven need not be a part of the house at all – a pavilion, gazebo or summerhouse in a rambling garden has a natural seclusion and a romantic atmosphere all its own.

A sheltered terrace or patio, as an extension of the house, enhances both the surroundings outside and adds a sense of space and light inside, perhaps echoing the prevailing style of the interior. An air of balanced, classical harmony will pervade a leafy arbour of orange trees ranged to either side in terracotta urns with cool glazed tiles underfoot. A patio roofed with an informal tangle of roses and honeysuckle becomes an oasis of fragrant exotica with the addition of pink oleander and china-blue plumbago – the perfect corner for a romantic picnic of strawberries and cream. Potted plants provide a moveable feast of colour and foliage.

Scope for a garden can be found within the house itself: a sunny landing or even a window seat can become an indoor garden which flowers all year round. Take up the theme with a leafy wallpaper and floral fabric. Fragrant jasmine or honeysuckle grown outside and trained around the window will scent evening breezes. A balcony or roof garden, furnished with a profusion of plants and flowers, will create an *al fresco* touch.

The very nature of a garden room, with its abundance of fragrant flowers and foliage, creates a romantic environment, an indoor garden of earthly delights. It can be a flower-filled setting for summer entertaining, the air heavy with exotic scent, or for lazy afternoons, redolent of Edwardian summers, spent curled up in a fringed hammock with a novel and a lace parasol.

The earliest garden rooms were built in the seventeenth century as orangeries to protect exotic fruit trees. A conservatory which linked the drawing-room to the garden provided a perfect bridge with nature in keeping with Picturesque sensibilities; conservatories were even built to adjoin ladies' boudoirs so they could walk amongst exotic blooms at all times of day regardless of inclement weather. The extravagant cast-iron and glass structures of Paxton's conservatories at Chatsworth and Crystal Palace inspired the winter gardens of the Victorians, in which rare plants, transplanted home from adventurous forays abroad, could be nurtured.

The aura of the classic Victorian conservatory can be recreated with a tropical jungle of ferns and foliage, wrought-iron furniture plied with floral chintz cushions and jardinières filled with scented parma violets. Or conjure the romantic atmosphere of an Edwardian verandah with basket loungers in which to enjoy the noonday sun, shaded by awnings or an edible canopy of luscious grape vines.

The pleasures of such an oasis can be enjoyed come rain or shine; the perfect place to celebrate the golden days of summer or a scented haven on winter days when snow lies deep.

INDEX

Numbers in italics refer to illustrations

ACKNOWLEDGEMENTS

The publishers wish to thank the following for permission to reproduce the illustrations: Boys Syndication p 20 right, p 23 right, p 43, p 46, p 47, p 59, p 70, p 73, p 87. Bridgeman Art Library, London, with acknowledgement to: Private Collections p 10, 34 (inset), 44, 96; Cheltenham Art Gallery and Museums, Gloucestershire p 20 left; Musée d'Orsay, Paris p 33; Oldham Art Gallery, Lancashire p 41, 108; Roy Miles Fine Paintings, London p 50; Gavin Graham Gallery, London p 58 above; Musée des Beaux-Arts, Tourcoing pp 64–5; Agnew & Sons, London p 66; Christie's, London p 69, pp 100–101; Guildhall Art Gallery, London pp 74–5; Forbes Magazine Collection, New York p 78; Anthony Mitchell, Nottinghamshire p 83. Published by the Bucentaur Gallery Ltd, London, as a greeting card p 89. Linda Burgess/Insight p 81, pp 88–9, pp 96–7. Christie's Colour Library, London p 27. Fine Arts Photographic Library, London p 95. Garden Picture Library, London p 91, photos Guy Bouchet p 14 (inset) and p 19 (inset). John Glover p 58 below. Mick Hales p 12, p 32, p 94. Photographs by Fritz von der Schulenburg pp 10–11, p 83, p 103, p 109, and with acknowledgements to Christophe Gollut/Pierre-Marie Rudelle (trompe l'oeil)

pp 6–7; Barbara Thornhill/The Egyptian Suite at the Halcyon Hotel, London pp 8–9; Mimi O'Connell/Peter Farlow (stencil) pp 16–17; David Hicks p 24 left; Kelly Hoppen p 25; David Hicks/courtesy Country Homes and Interiors pp 36–7; Miguel Servera, Majorca p 39 above; Victoria Waymouth p 39 centre; Conrad Jamieson p 39 below; Andrea de Montal p 48, pp 54–5; Karl Lagerfeld p 53; Willa Elphinstone pp 56–7; Sisi Edmiston p 63, p 99; Kenneth Turner/Library, Osterley Park p 71; Nicole de Fayet/Chateau de Montmirail, Le Mans p 82; Stephen Falk p 90; Janet Fitch p 105. Elizabeth Whiting & Associates, London, photographs by: Andreas Von Einsiedel pp 18–19, 51, with Pauline Boardman pp 14–15, p 45, p 93, with Charmat p 102, with Biggs p 21, with Nicholas Haslam pp 30–31; Michael Nicholson p 17, with Virginia Bates p 36, p 38; Spike Powell pp 22–3, p 62, with Bella Campbell pp 34–35; Jerry Tubby p 26, with Jill Hudson p 40, p 42; Neil Lorimer p 28 left, p 86; Michael Crockett p 29; Steve Colby/Cass Thomas p 49; Michael Dunne p 52, p 72, p 80, with Nicholas Garrett p 67; Di Lewis p 60, p 79, p 84, p 85, p 92; Tom Leighton p 68, p 104; Victoria Watts pp 76–7; Jerry Harpur pp 106–7.

LIST OF PAINTINGS

George Clausen, *The Visit* (detail) p 10; Leonard Campbell-Taylor, *Interior* p 20; John Lavery, *Spring* p 33; Alice Squire, *Young Woman in an Attic Bedroom* p 34; Patrick William Adam, *Interior, Morning* (detail) p 41; John Singer Sargent, *Mrs Carl Meyer, later Lady Meyer, and her two Children* p 44; Georges Croegaert, *La Liseuse* (detail) p 50; Albert Breaute, *Woman in an Interior* (detail) p 58 above; Jules Alexandre Grun, *The End of Dinner* p 64–5; Marcus Stone, *A Woman by a Fireside* (detail) p 66; Carlton Alfred Smith, *Home* p 69; J.J.J. Tissot, *Too Early* pp 74–5; Jessica Hayllar, *A Coming Event* p 78; Jacques Cancaret, *Repose* (detail) p 83; Charles Haigh-Wood, *Fair Deceivers* (detail) p 95; Pierre Joseph Redouté, *Forgetmenots* p 96; J.J.J. Tissot, *In The Conservatory (The Rivals)* pp 100–101; Philip Connard, *A Chelsea Interior* p 108.